ALLOWING GOD TO WRITE YOUR LOVE STORY

Tools for Women Thriving in Their Singleness

Dr. Tawanda Lawrence

ISBN 979-8-88851-833-5 (Paperback)
ISBN 979-8-88851-834-2 (Digital)

Covenant Books
11661 Hwy 707
Murrells Inlet, SC 29576
www.covenantbooks.com

In loving memory of my aunt, Annie Ruth.

Thank you for letting your light shine in our family and always showing up. You did not receive the opportunity to read this book, but I know you would have been first in line to show your support!

CONTENTS

PROLOGUE

Welcome to all my single sisters! Whether you are twenty-five or fifty-five, if you desire to be married and have been waiting for a while, this book is for you! I am a Christian, educated, Black woman who has never been married, with no children, at the age of forty-seven. I struggled with being single for many years of my adult life. I always thought marriage would be a natural course of events and simply fall into place for me. Can you imagine my surprise when the fairy-tale ending to the love story I always dreamed of did not occur the way I planned? I found myself feeling disappointed, frustrated, and confused.

I always had the desire to write an inspirational book for single women. Initially, I thought my book would be written from the perspective of a married woman sharing lessons learned throughout my singleness, but God had a different plan. In 2022, I had a revelation that the book I always wanted to write should not be put on hold. I thought, *Why should I wait until I am married?* Although I am still waiting to receive the promise of marriage that God has placed in my heart, the message I have to share could be the encouragement another woman needs to hear now. Writing this book has brought me so much joy! The most fulfilling part about this mission is that my motivation was to share tools with other single women, but the more I wrote, the more I realized that I was actually ministering to myself. This book reminds me that I continue to be a work in progress as I learn, grow, and develop in my singleness.

In September 2020, *Psychology Today* posted a startling article written by Dr. Bella DePaulo titled "Record Number of Americans

Have Never Married and Never Will." In this article, Dr. DePaulo discusses the 2014 data-based prediction by the Pew Research Center that indicated the likelihood a person will marry in the United States will depend on their age. According to this article, the Pew Research Center predicts the number of women and men ages twenty-five to thirty-four who married over a twelve-month period is seventy-one out of a thousand. This research also reveals that the opportunity for marriage quickly declines as a person gets older, for example, ages forty-five to fifty-four is sixteen out of one thousand and ages fifty-five and older is seven out of a thousand.

Although these statistics are disheartening, the Word of God tells us the opposite about marriage. In Genesis 2:18, God said, "It is not good for the man to be alone. I will make a helper suitable for him." Scripture also states, "He who finds a wife finds what is good and receives favor from the LORD" (Proverbs 18:22). A wife is described to have noble character, and "Her husband has full confidence in her and lacks nothing of value. She brings him good, not harm, all the days of her life" (Proverbs 31:11–12). There is a preponderance of literature, research studies, and data reports that signify the institution of marriage is not valued in today's society, but marriage is and will always be honorable in God's sight.

This book explores the thoughts, feelings, and emotions that many single women face on their journey toward marriage, and my prayer is that it provides tools and strategies that can be applied as you continue to wait for God. The content of this book contains various lessons I have gathered throughout my life beginning with the values my loving parents, Willie and Barbara Lawrence, instilled in me since childhood. I have also been encouraged by the messages I have received from spiritual leaders, Senior Pastor Reginald Sharpe Jr. and Pastor Emeritus Charles Jenkins of Fellowship Missionary Baptist Church, where I am a faithful member in Chicago. I have also been influenced by the biblical teachings of many others such as Pastors Joel Osteen, Bill Winston, Joyce Meyer, T. D. Jakes, and Jerry Flowers.

As you read this book, you will notice it is divided into four sections. Each of the four sections focuses on the various elements of a story. The main parts of every story typically consist of five basic elements (characters, setting, plot, conflict, and resolution), and great authors understand how to utilize these story elements to create a memorable story. I was intentional about structuring the book in this way because if we truly allow God, who is the greatest author, to write our love story, we must give him space to write every part of our story from the characters to the resolution. Each section will begin with a Launch Activity to prepare you for the content you will explore and conclude with a Closing Activity that will allow you to reflect on information you read.

My prayer is that this book will bless you with practical tools to help transform how you approach your journey toward marriage. Allowing God to write your love story will require you to take a step back to provide room for God to step in and do his work in your life. With God as the author of your love story, you will *stop living* in your singleness and *start thriving* in your singleness!

THE AUTHOR: OMNIPOTENCE

I am the LORD, the God of all mankind.
Is anything too hard for me?
—Jeremiah 32:27

The omnipotence of God is so amazing! Our heavenly Father has authority over everything, and his supreme power has no limitations. If you believe that God is the source and provider for all your needs, your love story should not be excluded. Allowing God to write your love story signifies that you have turned over every aspect of your journey toward marriage to him, which in essence gives God the authority to author the who, what, how, when, and where according to his will.

If you have yearned for marriage, and it has not happened for you after years of waiting, it may be difficult to give God complete control of your love story. At times, there can be an urge to hold on tightly to the things you desire most. But our Creator is more powerful than any issue or problem, and he has the authority to bring your desires to pass. When you choose to allow God to write your love story, you acknowledge God as your source and recognize that you cannot make things happen on your own. If you have been single and waiting for your husband longer than you planned, most likely you have tried things your way for quite some time. In Matthew 6:33, Jesus says, "But seek first his kingdom and his righteousness, and all these things will be given to you as well." This scripture teaches the first step is to put God first, not second or last, but first. Embrace

God's omnipotence and give him control over your love story by seeking him through prayer, faith, and gratitude.

God wants his children to spend time with him in prayer. Prayer is simply a conversation with God, an opportunity to thank God for all he has done and make your requests known to him. Because our God has supreme authority over everything, and he wants the best for you, ask him for exactly what you want according to his will. Do not be afraid to pray big and bold prayers! Ask God for the things you cannot do on your own, but with him, these things are possible! Making your requests known to God is only the beginning. The next step, which at times is overlooked, is the belief that you have received what you asked for when you pray. Jesus told the disciples in Mark 11:23–24:

> Truly I tell you, if anyone says to the mountain, "Go, throw yourself into the sea," and does not doubt in their heart but believes that what they say will happen, it will be done for them. Therefore I tell you, whatever you ask for in prayer, believe that you have received it, and it will be yours.

After you have made your request for marriage known to God, and you believe you have received what you asked for is when your faith in the omnipotence of our God has to kick in. *Merriam-Webster* defines faith as "belief and trust in and loyalty to God, something that is believed especially with strong conviction." Having faith in something you cannot see is not easy, and your faith might be tested while you are waiting for your love story to unfold. The waiting period will require unwavering faith, the kind of faith that allows you to know, without a shadow of a doubt, that God has not forgotten about you when your circumstances are not changing, and it seems as though your prayer is not being answered. Scripture states, "Now faith is confidence in what we hope for and assurance about what we do not see" (Hebrews 11:1). Make the decision to continue to believe that God is turning your situation around in your favor, despite what you see.

Showing gratitude to God and thanking him for all things must accompany your prayer and unwavering faith. While you have not received your desire to be married *yet*, God has granted so many blessings in your life that should be acknowledged. Continue to thank God for the strength he has provided you along the way, his protection over your life, and the grace, mercy, and favor he continues to bestow upon you. Give thanks to God now! Thank him in advance for all he has planned for your love story. Thank God in the present for your future husband that is making his way to you. Thank God at this moment that he is preparing you to be a wife. Finally, thank God today, tomorrow, and next week that he is getting your husband ready for you every day!

PART 1

CHARACTERS

Characters

The characters are the most significant element of a story. The *primary character* is the lead role in which a storyline is centered on. Your favorite novel, television show, or movie has a primary character in which the storyline is focused. Whether the literary genre is fiction or nonfiction or the film is comedy or romance, one of the qualities that may have drawn you to the primary character is the way in which the character navigated the twists and turns in the storyline.

You may be wondering how this connects to your life. Our heavenly Father is in control of all things. He is the author and composer of your love story, and *you* are the primary character in the love story God has created for you. Similar to a primary character in a television series, musical, or short story, your love story is based on your experiences, your point of view and perspectives, as well as your reactions to all life brings. Take a few minutes to think about how you have been showing up as the primary character in your love story?

In addition to a primary character in a storyline, there is a *secondary character* who interacts with the primary character and assumes a supporting role. The secondary characters are crucial to the storyline because they contribute to the primary character's experiences. Can you think of a secondary character that you related to in a book you read or movie you watched? Most likely your connection with this character was based on how the person engaged with the primary character in the story. The secondary characters in your love story could be your love interests, family members, friends, or mentors. Who are the secondary characters in your life? How are they impacting your love story?

Part 1 of this book will provide the space for you to reflect on your role as the primary character in your love story and challenge you to consider the roles the secondary characters have played in your love story. Before we jump into the first chapter, it is important that you complete the Launch Activity.

Part 1: Launch Activity

What are the most challenging things about being a single woman?	*How* have you navigated these challenges?	*When* have you received support from others during your challenging times as a single woman?

Overcomer

Consider it pure joy, my brothers and sisters, whenever you face trials of many kinds, because you know that the testing of your faith produces perseverance. Let perseverance finish its work so that you may be mature and complete, not lacking anything.

—James 1:2–4

Life is filled with trials and tribulations. In the midst of the many challenges life may bring, being single is often a major obstacle for women who desire marriage. Singleness can result in many emotions that cause a woman who yearns to be married to feel sad, angry, and scared. The longer the wait, the more these feelings can fester and evolve into loneliness, inferiority, hostility, frustration, anxiety, jealousy, and embarrassment.

Putting yourself out there to meet new people, opening your heart to love when it has been broken over and over again, giving second and sometimes third chances, raising your standards and even lowering your standards can be exhausting. Blind dates, dating sites, speed dating, reconnections, new connections, hookups, ghosting, breadcrumbing, and the next new thing single women have to navigate in the world of dating may leave you disheartened. After all you have done and endured, the outcome remains the same. When you submit a survey or complete paperwork at the doctor's office, you find yourself checking the single box at the age of thirty, thirty-five, forty, forty-five.

In the book of James, the brother of Jesus teaches us to count it all joy when we encounter trials because in the testing of our faith, we will gain perseverance and be complete without lacking anything. As a believer, you most likely receive this message, but let's be real, considering trials to be joy can be a challenge when you're in the struggle, right? When you are in the thick of it, I mean, really in it, you may feel like your trials are happening to you, but in actuality, they are happening for you. Your obstacles, barriers, and stumbling blocks help to build your character, strength, and endurance.

If you are reading this book, it is possible that you have experienced your share of good and bad relationships. As the primary character in your love story, you are an *overcomer*. You overcame the man who walked away from you, the unfaithfulness, the absence of the father of your child, the lies, deceit, and abuse. You are an overcomer because you did not allow those negative circumstances to defeat you. You prevailed in spite of these hardships. Take a moment to celebrate yourself for being an overcomer.

The fact that you are still here is a testament that God has greater things in store for you. The pain you have endured or currently experiencing is not in vain. God has a purpose for your life, and the love story he is writing for you is going to be *amazing*! All your suffering will not matter when God's plan for your life comes together. We find this promise in Job 8:7, and it says, "Your beginnings will seem humble, so prosperous will your future be." So make the decision to leave the past in the past, stop thinking and talking about it, burn it, lock it, and throw away the key. Focus on what lies ahead. God has prepared an amazing future for you that will not be lacking anything, including the husband you desire!

Allies

As iron sharpens iron, so one person sharpens another.
— Proverbs 27:17

The secondary characters are instrumental to any storyline. There are times when the secondary character serves as an ally to the primary character. As an ally, the secondary character's role is to support and help the primary character achieve the goal. Just as there is an ally, oftentimes, there is an adversary. The adversary is a secondary character that is the complete opposite of an ally. Their role is a source of conflict for the primary character and attempts to prevent the primary character from achieving the goal. Scripture teaches that iron sharpens iron, which describes how important it is that the people we invite into our lives have a positive impact on our story.

As you journey through life, you will encounter many different people; some of whom you will build close relationships that evolve into a circle or network of family members, friends, spiritual leaders, colleagues, neighbors, mentors, counselors, etc. God created his children to establish relationships and be in community with each other. We find this promise in Ecclesiastes 4:9–10, which states:

> Two are better than one, because they have
> a good return for their labor: If either of them
> falls down, one can help the other up. But pity
> anyone who falls and has no one to help them up.

God does not intend for you to journey through your life without a support system to embrace, enlighten, edify, and encourage you.

At the beginning of "Part 1" in this book, you completed a Launch Activity that allowed you to reflect on the challenges of being a single woman and how the people in your life have supported you. As God is writing your love story, it is important that the people in your circle or network are secondary characters serving as allies and not adversaries. Be cognizant of the adversaries in your life, who present themselves or appear to be supportive of your story, but deep down they are jealous and fear your success or progress. Allies believe that God has the best for you. They are honest, dependable, trustworthy, loyal, and live with integrity. Of course, no relationship is perfect, but throughout the ups and downs, disagreements, and misunderstandings, an ally loves and cares for you and genuinely wants you to win.

In Matthew 18:19–20, Jesus says:

> Again, truly I tell you that if two of you on earth agree about anything they ask for, it will be done for them by my Father in heaven. For where two or three gather in my name, there am I with them.

According to this verse, if any two of you agree, God will fulfill his promise for what you are believing. While you are waiting for God to unveil your love story, find a prayer partner who will be in agreement with the promise God has placed in your heart about marriage. *Agreement* is the operative word in this verse. Your prayer partner must believe, despite what it looks like and beyond all circumstances, that God is in the process of bringing your husband to you, someone who does not have any doubt or disbelief about God's promise.

There are clear benefits to having a support system, but if you do not currently have a network of people who serve as allies in your love story, there is no need to be concerned or worried. Continue to seek God for guidance, and he will ensure that the right people come into your life. You are not alone. In Isaiah 41:10, God says, "So do not fear, for I am with you; do not be dismayed, for I am your God. I will strengthen you and help you; I will uphold you with my righteous right hand."

As you come to the end of "Part 1" in this book, you should complete the Closing Activity before proceeding to the next section.

Part 1: Closing Activity

"Part 1" examines the author of your love story and the characters in your love story. As you move toward allowing God to write your love story, identify an *insight*—one big idea you are taking away from each chapter in "Part 1" and an *implication*—why the area of focus is significant for you.

Chapter	Insight	Implication
Omnipotence		
Overcomer		
Allies		

PART 2

SETTING, PLOT, and CONFLICT

Setting

The setting connects the reader to the time, place, and environment of the story. A story does not exist without a physical place. Every storyline has a setting that allows the audience to immerse themselves in the time and location in which the narrative is being told. The setting is an essential element of the storyline that makes the story more interesting as events are often visualized through illustrations in a children's book, props on a theater stage, or an aerial shot of a scene in a film.

The next two chapters of this book will explore how God creates the setting for your love story. As the author, he establishes when and where your husband will enter your life. As you get ready to embark upon "Part 2" of this book, take a few minutes to answer the questions in the Launch Activity.

Part 2: Launch Activity

1) **How has time impacted how you feel about your singleness?**

2) **In what ways have you attempted to control the outcome of your romantic relationships?**

3) **How have the disappointments you experienced in past relationships impacted how you view your singleness?**

Time

For the revelation awaits an appointed time. It speaks of
the end and will not prove false. Though it linger, wait
for it; it will certainly come and will not delay.

—Habakkuk 2:3

The "biological clock is ticking," "life is short," and "time flies by" are just a few phrases that can cause a single woman to believe there is an urgency for things to happen immediately in her life. Depending on how long you have been waiting for God to fulfill your desire for marriage, you may have experienced moments in your journey when you have felt you are falling behind. According to your plan, you should have been married years ago! Many people have often wondered, and some have boldly asked, "Why are you single?" There may have been moments when you secretly questioned yourself as well. You possess all the qualities and characteristics that will make you a great wife, so why is it taking so long for marriage to happen for you?

When you allow God to be the author of your love story, he creates the setting of the story, which includes when and where your love story will be revealed. Scripture states, "He has made everything beautiful in its time. He has also set eternity in the human heart; yet no one can fathom what God has done from beginning to end" (Ecclesiastes 3:11). God's timing will not always correlate with your schedule or calendar of events, which could require more time for your desires to come to pass than you anticipated. When God's timing is not aligned with your plans, it may cause you to believe that nothing is happening because you do not see the evidence of things coming together. You could feel like you are at a standstill and making no progress toward marriage. During these times, it is imperative that your faith kicks into overdrive, and you trust that God is using this time to put things in order for your favor. The time that appears to be stalled or lagging behind, God is orchestrating the perfect place, time, and opportunity for everything to come together.

In this day and age, a microwave society exists where there is a mindset of wanting everything now and without wait time. The way in which technology has evolved provides an instant gratification that transfers to many aspects of life, including romantic relationships. The impulse of requiring things to happen according to your timeline can result in forcing relationships and situations to happen on your own accord. Making the decision to get involved in relationships without seeking God, trying hard to make someone like you, and manipulating situations for your benefit are only a few actions that will take you out of God's timing. God's plan for your life is so much better than your plan so try not to force things to happen on your own terms because you feel the pressure of time passing you by. Your love story will come together beautifully at God's appointed time.

In a calendar year, there are twelve months, fifty-two weeks, 365 days, 8,670 hours, and 525,600 minutes. Although time does not stop for anyone or anything, all that God has for you will not go to anyone but you and will not be a millisecond late. This promise is found in 1 Corinthians 2:9, which states, "However, as it is written: 'What no eye has seen, what no ear has heard, and what no human mind has conceived' the things God has prepared for those who love him." Time is not a factor for what God has prepared for you!

Seasons

There is a time for everything, and a season for every activity under the heavens: a time to be born and a time die, a time to plant and a time to uproot, a time to kill and a time to heal, a time to tear down and a time to build, a time to weep and a time to laugh, a time to mourn and a time to dance, a time to scatter stones and a time to gather them, a time to embrace and a time to refrain from embracing, a time to search and a time to give up, a time to keep and a time to throw away, a time to tear and a time to mend, a time to be silent and a time to speak, a time to love and a time to hate, a time for war and a time for peace.

—Ecclesiastes 3:1–8

In 1981, Jim Rohn wrote *The Seasons of Life*, a popular book that compared the seasons of nature to personal seasons people experience in life. According to Rohn, the personal seasons in life encompass winter in which despair, loneliness, and disappointment are prevalent, while hope and new opportunities emerge in spring. Growth, strength, and development occur in the personal season of summer, and reward, achievement, and celebration evolve in fall. Similarly, Ecclesiastes 3:1–8 explains, for everything there is a season. It is inevitable that in life, you will experience good and bad times, moments where there is darkness balanced with times when the sun shines brightly.

When you give God the pen to write your love story, he has the authority to design each season of your life and decide when it is time for you to move from one season to another. This is the part of the setting in which the author creates the environment of the story to depict the surroundings that may include the physical landscape, weather, and societal and cultural circumstances. The author influences how the setting develops throughout the story. As a single woman, you may find yourself in the personal season of winter where you feel lonely and desire companionship longer than you anticipated. Although this season seems like it will never end, it is not permanent. No season remains the same forever. During this season, it is important that you accept where you are without becoming resentful, and God will move you into the personal season of summer, where you experience growth, preparing you for the personal season of fall where you will receive all God has in store for you.

In 2 Corinthians 4:18, Paul writes, "So we fix our eyes not on what is seen, but on what is unseen, since what is seen is temporary, but what is unseen is eternal." *Your singleness is temporary.* Again, for those who missed it the first time, *your singleness is temporary.* One last time, in case you did not think that message was meant for you, *your singleness is temporary.* If you focus on what you see, it is easy to believe that being single is the way your life will always be when your status is not changing. Do not allow your emotions to get the best of you. What you see is subject to change as God transitions you into a new season. Focus on God's love and goodness, which is permanent and will not fail, no matter what season you are in.

Persevere through the challenging times, maintain a positive attitude, and prepare yourself for the new season God has for you. The season you will enter to receive all God has for you will be more than you ever expected and worth every season you endured to get there. Scripture confirms, "Let us not become weary in doing good, for at the proper time we will reap a harvest if we do not give up" (Galatians 6:9).

Plot

Every compelling story has a plot. The plot is what actually happens in the story and how the storyline unfolds. The what, the how, the why, and the result. The plot takes the reader or audience on a journey of the sequence of events, from the beginning to the end of the story. Each event creates a broader narrative in which a series of causes and effects shape the story. Cause-and-effect allows the story to evolve as one event leads to another event.

The author of the story develops and writes the plot. This includes the sequence of events and the cause-and-effect circumstances the primary character experiences. In essence, the author of the story is in complete control of what happens in the story and how the story happens. The next chapter will explore how God, as the author, develops the plot of your love story. When God writes your love story, he orchestrates the chain of events that will bring you to where you need to be according to his plan.

Surrender

He says, "Be still, and know that I am God, I will be exalted
among the nations, I will be exalted in the earth."

—Psalm 46:10

To surrender to God involves completely giving up your
thoughts, ideas, and plans to the will of God. It requires you to relinquish control of your life to our heavenly Father. Every day, you make
hundreds of choices for your life. You choose what you are going to
eat for breakfast, you plan your agenda for the day, you determine
the route you will take to get to work, and you decide how you will
spend your free time, just to name a few. All the decisions you make
in a fraction of a second could lead you to believe that you are in control of what happens in your life. Scripture explains, "Many are the
plans in a person's heart, but it is the Lord's purpose that prevails"
(Proverbs 19:21). God has planned our days from beginning to end,
and in Jeremiah 29:11, God's children are reminded of this, "'For I
know the plans I have for you,' declares the Lord, 'plans to prosper
you and not to harm you, plans to give you hope and a future.'"

God's plan for your love story is much greater than any plan
you could ever create. Imagine God telling you to *turn over all worries and fears* you have about being lonely, *release the frustrations* that
are bottled up inside about failed relationships, *hand over the anxiety*
you experience when things are not going the way you have planned,
render the disappointment of not having closure at the end of a relationship, and *let go of the insecurities* about not being good enough
or worthy of love. Imagine God telling you to *stop trying to figure it
out* and *stop forcing things to happen.* God does not want his children
to be burdened. In Matthew 11:28–30, Jesus states, "Come to me,
all you who are weary and burdened, and I will give you rest. Take
my yoke upon you and learn from me, for I am gentle and humble in
heart, and you will find rest for your souls. For my yoke is easy and
my burden is light."

Make the decision *today* to release complete control of how your love story comes to pass, and trust that God knows what is best for you. When you truly surrender control to God, it will feel like a weight has been lifted off your shoulders, you are more relaxed because you have taken the pressure off yourself, and you are at peace with God ordering your steps.

In Psalm 46:10, God advises his children to be still and know that he is God. In just a few words, God is relaying a clear message that you cannot make things happen on your own; so step back, I got this! How many times have you been frustrated about your singleness because you tried to control things you were not supposed to control? In this scripture, God is reminding his children to believe in his plan. When you allow God to write your love story, you give him permission to work out his plan for your love story, including the plot that contains every event from beginning to end.

Surrendering requires you to allow God to orchestrate the chain of events in your love story without intervening when things are not going your way. As the primary character, you are experiencing your love story in real time, and each event you encounter is isolated. While in the moment, it is difficult to understand that everything, good and bad, is working for your good, but when God completes your love story, you will see there was a purpose for everything you experienced. It is liberating when you make the choice to let go and let God. Trust that his plan is the best approach to get you where you need to be.

Conflict

Conflict arises in every story to create obstacles for the primary character to overcome. Various forms of conflict enter the story to interfere with the primary character achieving their goal. These challenges appear in the storyline to get in the way of what the person wants or needs. A film, musical, or novel would most likely be less intriguing without some form of conflict. The conflict brings entertainment value to the story as it engages the reader or viewer and builds an emotional response.

The author of a story creates conflict to establish barriers or stumbling blocks for the primary character to push through. As the primary character in your love story, most likely you have encountered various challenges on your journey toward marriage. The final chapters in "Part 2" of this book will present ways in which conflict may emerge as God continues to author your love story.

Waiting

I wait for the Lord, my whole being
waits, and in his word I put my hope.
—Psalm 130:5

Waiting is hard. *Period.* Waiting can be challenging when it comes to the simple things you experience day-to-day, such as waiting in a long line at the grocery store, waiting for a person to respond to an email you sent two days ago, or waiting at a railroad crossing as a train passes by. Waiting can be grueling if you have been waiting years or even decades for your heart's desire to come to pass. Waiting is one of many conflicts that may arise while God is writing your love story. Waiting can produce a major barrier for you to push through on your journey toward marriage. As a single woman, it is possible that someone or multiple people have told you to "wait on God." By telling you to "wait on God," in all likelihood, their intention was to encourage and remind you that God is in control. As a believer, you are more than aware that God is in control. The question that often remains is how do you practice patience when you have an intense longing to be married? What does "wait on God" look and sound like?

In Psalm 130:5, the writer explains that his whole being waits for the Lord, and his hope is in the Word of God. Patience requires a shift in how you respond while in the waiting period. The longer your wait time, the more your patience will be tested. During this time, a shift in your whole being is necessary as it relates to your thoughts, words, and actions. Although what your eyes see may create thoughts of disbelief and negativity, fill your mind with positive thoughts as you put your hope in the promises of God. "Finally, brothers and sisters, whatever is true, whatever is noble, whatever is right, whatever is pure, whatever is lovely, whatever is admirable—if anything is excellent or praiseworthy—think about such things" (Philippians 4:8).

Your circumstances may cause you to complain about your situation not changing, but be careful of the words you speak. "Anxiety weighs down the heart, but a kind word cheers it up" (Proverbs 12:25). In the face of frustration, as you wait, year after year, discover ways to cope and protect your peace. "You will keep in perfect peace those whose minds are steadfast, because they trust in you" (Isaiah 26:3).

During the waiting period, it is easy to believe that nothing is happening because your circumstances have remained the same. You might think that God has forgotten about you because most of your friends have gotten married and you have been waiting so long. It may seem like nothing is happening, but the waiting period is actually the most important part of the journey because God is not only writing the most beautiful and rewarding love story for you, he is also developing who you are in the process. God is doing a great work in you and for you! God is preparing you for what he has in store for you. He is building your character, strength, courage, endurance, and attitude as you continue to be faithful to him by making the right choices when your prayers have not been answered. You are becoming a better version of yourself, so embrace the process, despite how long it takes.

Scripture states, "Being confident of this, that he who began a good work in you will carry it on to completion until the day of Christ Jesus" (Philippians 1:6).

Detours

Not only so, but we also glory in our sufferings, because we
know that suffering produces perseverance; perseverance,
character; and character, hope. And hope does not put us
to shame, because God's love has been poured out into our
hearts through the Holy Spirit, who has been given to us.

—Romans 5:3–5

Another conflict you may encounter during your journey toward marriage will include countless detours. Life is not a path that looks like a straight line. Instead, it is a path with arrows that point up, down, left, and right. There may be moments when you think your life is moving in one direction, and you encounter a roadblock that forces you to change course. This alternate route was not one of the steps in the list of directions you intended to follow to get from point A to point B. But many times, the detours you run into along your journey are a part of God's plan to guide you closer to the destination he has for you. The roadblocks will not prevent you from getting to your destination if you do not cancel the route guidance. Hold on to your faith, and trust that your heavenly Father has a better route for you to travel and keep moving forward. God speaks of this in Isaiah 55:8–9, and he says:

> "For my thoughts are not your thoughts,
> neither are your ways my ways," declares the
> LORD. "As the heavens are higher than the earth,
> so are my ways higher than your ways and my
> thoughts than your thoughts."

As a single woman, you may have endured many failed relationships that caused you pain, relationships that you thought were on track and moving in the right direction. These disappointments may have left you heartbroken and discouraged, but God has a purpose for everything that happens in your life. He would not have allowed the detours if they were going to prevent you from getting to the destination he has for you. If your love story is not turning out the way you planned, learn from the lessons in each unfortunate situation and allow those lessons to develop your character. The challenges are necessary to prepare you for all that God has in store for you. "And we know that in all things God works for the good of those who love him, who have been called according to his purpose" (Romans 8:28). *All* things work together for good, not some things, not just the good things, but *all* things, which includes the unpleasant situations you would rather bypass.

When traveling to a destination, detours typically add more travel time, and it may feel like you are going in the wrong direction because the alternate route was not your original plan. Detours are a part of the process, but rerouting can be uncomfortable, confusing, and unpredictable. What seems like a barrier in your journey toward marriage, God will use for your advantage. Continue to stand in your faith and believe that the delay is allowing God to prepare you for his best. Trust God's direction, and allow him to order your steps. In Psalm 37:23–24, the writer declares:

> The LORD makes firm the steps of the one
> who delights in him; though he may stumble, he
> will not fall, for the LORD upholds him with his
> hand.

Now that you have reached the end of "Part 2" in this book, reflect on the chapters in this section and complete the Closing Activity below, before proceeding to "Part 3."

Part 2: Closing Activity

"Part 2" identifies how God creates the setting, writes the plot, and allows conflict to arise during your journey toward marriage. Revisit your answers to the three questions in the Launch Activity at the beginning of "Part 2." Reflect on the chapters you read in "Part 2" and return to this Closing Activity to identify three things you learned, two interesting facts, and one lingering question you have.

Three things I learned.

<table>
<tr><td></td><td></td><td></td></tr>
</table>

Two facts I found interesting.

<table>
<tr><td></td><td></td></tr>
</table>

One question I have.

<table>
<tr><td></td></tr>
</table>

PART 3

THEME

Theme

The theme is the central idea or meaning behind the story contingent on what the characters learned and how they changed. It is often considered the point of the story or an important idea that is embedded throughout the story. The theme gives significance but is not stated directly. It is explored through the different elements of a story like the characters, plot, settings, and conflict. There are various types of themes that authors may convey in a story. A few familiar themes are: coming of age—involves the experiences of growing up; good versus evil—delves into the conflict between good and evil; and identity—explores the question, who am I?

Two themes that may emerge as God writes your love story are the pursuit of love and faith versus doubt. The pursuit of love—acknowledges that love is beautiful but can be challenging to find as conflict often arises when pursuing it. Faith versus doubt—confronts the moments when your faith in God will be tested, and believing is not always easy. The chapters in "Part 3" will help you to navigate these two themes. Before you dive into "Part 3" of this book, complete the Launch Activity.

Part 3: Launch Activity

Describe how you associate the terms below with your singleness.

Contentment	
Purpose	
Happiness	

Contentment

I am not saying this because I am in need, for I have learned
to be content whatever the circumstances. I know what it is
to be in need, and I know what it is to have plenty. I have
learned the secret of being content in any and every situation,
whether well fed or hungry, whether living in plenty or in
want. I can do all this through him who gives me strength.
—Philippians 4:11–13

The pursuit of love is the major theme in your love story. As God
unfolds your love story in his way and his timing, the theme of faith
versus doubt will emerge throughout your journey. As a believer, the
battle between faith and doubt can be disconcerting. You believe that
God has the power to do anything, but doubt creeps in when you do
not see evidence of marriage on the horizon. You proceed to analyze
how, and at times, if it is going to happen. During these times, it is
important to remember that God is the author of your love story, and
he will decide how it will come to pass.

In Philippians 4:11–13, the apostle Paul wrote that he learned
to be content in all situations and circumstances. Contentment is to
be at peace, not only when things are going your way but also partic-
ularly during the times when things are not working out according
to your plans. To be content means you are not worried about your
future because God is in control. Jesus asked, "Can any one of you
by worrying add a single hour to your life?" Simply put, worry, frustration, or pessimism will not change the situation. When it seems
as though you are farthest from the desires of your heart, continue to
maintain a positive attitude and show God that you trust his plan.

As your contentment continues to develop in your journey
toward marriage, *release, embrace,* and *trust.*

❖ *Release* the past. Let go of past mistakes, failed relationships, and plans that did not work out. It is difficult to

move forward in life when you are holding on to things of the past. You cannot change your past, and it has led you to where you are now. Give yourself permission to leave the past behind without any guilt or regrets.

❖ *Embrace* the present. Accept that God has you right where you are supposed to be. Every day you are blessed with life on this earth is a precious gift. Do not waste a minute of the present, wishing you were at a different place in your life. Be grateful for where you are. You will never have the opportunity to live today again.

❖ *Trust* God with your future. Have faith that your tomorrow is safe in God's hands. Believe that God has great things for you in the days to come. He is your heavenly Father who has protected and provided for you in the past and present. The omnipotence of God will not fail you in the future.

Purpose

For it is by grace you have been saved, through faith—and this is not from yourselves, it is the gift of God—not by works, so that no one can boast. For we are God's handiwork, created in Christ Jesus to do good works, which God prepared in advance for us to do.

—Ephesians 2:8–10

As God constructs the theme throughout your love story, the lessons you have learned and the ways in which you have changed during your journey toward marriage will emerge. God has a purpose for your life as a single woman. He has a plan for you before you become one with your husband. Use this time to develop a closer relationship with God, focus on the work you can do to build the kingdom of God, and develop your personal growth. Use this time wisely. Your singleness should not be in vain.

It is important that you are intentional about developing your relationship with God while you are single. Make God a priority by spending more time with him through prayer, worshipping him for all that he is, and reading and reflecting on his Word. Oftentimes, when a woman meets a man that she finds interesting, she will reserve time in her schedule to get to know him better. Building your relationship with God requires the same level of effort, if not more. Seek opportunities to draw closer to God every day until it becomes a routine. Your relationship with God is more important than any other relationship you will establish. It is the foundation for your life and should always come first. "For no one can lay any foundation other than the one already laid, which is Jesus Christ" (1 Corinthians 3:11).

As a single woman, God has given you additional time to do good work without the responsibilities that marriage brings. You have a role as a believer in the body of Christ to serve God and spread the Word of his goodness to others. Your heavenly Father has given you gifts and talents to use to advance his kingdom. This promise is found in 1 Corinthians 12:4–6, which states:

> There are different kinds of gifts, but the same Spirit distributes them. There are different kinds of service, but the same Lord. There are different kinds of working, but in all them and in everyone it is the same God at work.

If you are unsure of the work you have been called to do, ask God to reveal his purpose for your gifts and talents and the opportunities he has prepared for you to honor him during your season of singleness.

While you are building your relationship with God and exploring how you will honor God with your gifts and talents, embrace your singleness! Take this time to discover who you are as a woman.

Get to know yourself in the way that God sees you. David writes in Psalm 139:13–14:

> For you created my inmost being; you knit me together in my mother's womb. I praise you because I am fearfully and wonderfully made; your works are wonderful, I know that full well.

You are chosen by God and the apple of his eye. You are loved, valued, beautiful, kind, confident, important, accepted, resilient, worthy, and more than enough! Child of God, when you realize who you are and whose you are, your personal growth develops at a higher level. Where do you see yourself in the future? What are your personal, professional, and financial goals? Proverbs 21:5 explains, "The plans of the diligent lead to profit as surely as haste leads to poverty." Revisit the vision and goals you set for your life and establish actionable steps to fulfill your objectives. Create a vision board to display as a visual reminder of the goals you want to achieve, develop an action plan or checklist to help monitor your progress, and continue to pray that your goals are in alignment with God's will for your life. In Habakkuk 2:2, scripture states, "Then the Lord replied, 'Write down the revelation and make it plain on tablets so that a herald may run with it.'"

Happiness

> I keep my eyes always on the Lord. With him at my right hand, I will not be shaken. Therefore my heart is glad and my tongue rejoices; my body also will rest secure, because you will not abandon me to the realm of the dead, nor will you let your faithful one see decay.
>
> —Psalm 16:8–10

The pursuit of love is one of two major themes in your love story. The second theme that will most likely emerge is faith versus doubt. These are the moments when your faith in God to write your love story is tested. How you navigate these two themes is contingent on how you evolve and develop during your journey toward marriage. Have you become bitter or jealous? Is your spirit filled with joy? Are you miserable or discontent? Are you genuinely happy?

Your perspective has a huge impact on how your love story develops. Where you are at this point in your life is not an accident. You are exactly where God wants you to be. You may not have everything you desire, but you have everything you need with God, which is where your true happiness resides. Embrace God as your true source of happiness. He will be there for you no matter what happens in your life. In John 15:9–11, Jesus says:

> As the Father has loved me, so have I loved you. Now remain in my love. If you keep my commands, you will remain in my love, just as I have kept my Father's commands and remain in his love. I have told you this so that my joy may be in you and that your joy may be complete.

Being happy is easier said than done when life is not working out the way you anticipated. Creating your happiness wherever you are in your life is a choice. Make the decision to be happy, even if your love story is not working out your way. Life is precious, and every day is a blessing from God. Discover your happiness by engaging in activities that you enjoy. Here are ten ideas for you to consider as you continue to strengthen your happiness from the inside out.

❖ Fall in love with yourself.

❖ Speak positive affirmations over your life.

❖ Be comfortable with and in your silence. This is where self-awareness and self-reflection reside.

❖ Focus on your personal growth, and celebrate your progress.

❖   Slow down and embrace your journey.

❖   Spend quality time with yourself and get to know who you are and what you enjoy.

❖   Live your life, and don't put life on hold, waiting for your husband.

❖   Find ways to enjoy God's beautiful creation.

❖   Generate a list of activities you have never experienced, and do it.

❖   Be a help to someone in need.

Part 3: Closing Activity

"Part 3" addresses how God develops the theme as he is writing your love story. Revisit the Launch Activity at the beginning of "Part 3," and reflect on how you described the terms *contentment*, *purpose*, and *happiness* as they relate to your singleness. After reading this section, have your descriptions changed or remained the same? Identify one idea you found interesting in each chapter, and draw an image that will help you remember this key point.

Contentment	
Image	*Interesting Idea*
Purpose	
Image	*Interesting Idea*
Happiness	
Image	*Interesting Idea*

PART 4

RESOLUTION

Resolution

Every story—no matter how engaging, compelling, or captivating—has to come to an end. How the story ends for the primary and supporting characters matters a great deal to the reader or audience that is emotionally connected with the characters and invested in the outcome of the storyline. A resolution is the conclusion of the story's plot and allows the author to work out all main conflicts between the characters. The resolution will answer lingering questions and tie up loose ends in the story.

As the primary character in your love story, God will create a resolution that will bring you clarity, certainty, and comfort as you receive all that God has for you. Your love story will come together, and you will see that the challenges you encountered during your journey toward marriage brought you closer to the breakthrough. The last three chapters of this book will focus on God's resolution for your love story. Take some time to engage in the final Launch Activity.

Part 4: Launch Activity

Reflect on your favorite love story (novel, movie, play, or musical), and identify the primary character, setting, plot, conflict, and theme.

Favorite Love Story Title:	
Primary Character	
Setting	
Plot	
Conflict	
Theme	

Promise

Now I am about to go the way of all the earth. You
know with all your heart and soul that not one of all the
good promises the LORD your God gave you has failed.
Every promise has been fulfilled; not one has failed.

—Joshua 23:14

Statistics, research studies, self-help books, advice columns, blogs, YouTube videos, and relationship experts provide information and advice for women seeking marriage. Oftentimes, these resources are informative but, unfortunately, the guidance provided does not guarantee that if applied, your desire for marriage will come to pass. Are you seeking direction to help you navigate your journey toward marriage, instructions that have been proven over and over again to be successful, an absolute certainty that will not require a warranty or refund? If you allow God to write your love story, you will find every promise he has for your life in his Word. The promises God has embedded in Scripture will never fail in your life. He has the power and authority to deliver on every single promise. God's Word will come to pass, but you have to believe.

God created the concept of marriage because he recognized with Adam that it was not good for man to be alone, and Eve was created to be Adam's helper. Although God does not give the promise of marriage in the Bible, if you have a yearning to be married, God placed this desire in your heart and has called you to be married. Your desire for marriage is good because God honors marriage. As God concludes your love story, he will write a resolution that will bring to pass the desires of your heart. In Joshua 21:43–45, scripture reveals how God fulfilled the promises he made to the children of Israel:

So the LORD gave Israel all the land he had
sworn to give their ancestors, and they took pos-
session of it and settled there. The LORD gave

them rest on every side, just as he had sworn to their ancestors. Not one of their enemies withstood them; the LORD gave all their enemies into their hands. Not one of all the LORD's good promises to Israel failed; every one was fulfilled.

As you are waiting for God to develop your love story, it may take some time as the setting, theme, and plot evolve, so it will be important to remind yourself of the promises God has for you in his Word. Spend quality time reading the Bible and identify key scriptures to display as a visual reminder, recite as an affirmation, and reflect on through journaling and discussion with others. It is equally important that you remind God of his promises for you during your time with him. God, you promised (*insert your scripture here*). Heavenly Father, your Word teaches (*insert your scripture here*). God, you said (*insert your scripture here*). It is evident that God knows all things and has not forgotten about his promises, but reminding God will help you remember his promises when the wait gets hard and reassure you that God can be trusted to keep his Word as he resolves your love story.

Expectancy

Never be lacking in zeal, but keep your spiritual fervor, serving the LORD. Be joyful in hope, patient in affliction, faithful in prayer.
—Romans 12:11–12

God's conclusion to your love story will be found in the resolution where he will bring your journey toward marriage to completion, with the perfect ending. Your present circumstances may convey that your status remains single, but you have to believe that the man God has for you is in your future. You have come a long way in your journey, and the enemy will seek ways to convince you to lose hope. Do not allow your past disappointments, current circumstances, and future uncertainties cause you to stop believing that God has a great man in store for you.

Live in anticipation of God fulfilling your heart's desire, and maintain a high level of expectancy. Scripture confirms God's provision, which says:

> What, then, shall we say in response to these things? If God is for us, who can be against us? He who did not spare his own Son, but gave him up for us all—how will he not also, along with him, graciously give us all things?
> —Romans 8:31–32

Society will tell you to hope for the best but prepare for the worst to help ease the pain if things do not work out the way you planned. Expectancy is not only hope that what you desire is going to happen but also preparation for its arrival. In order to live with expectancy, it is important to think of positive thoughts, speak words of life into your future, and act in ways that reflect your preparation. Be consumed with hope that your husband is making his way to you, despite your circumstances, and continue to prepare for your situation to turn around every day because it can happen at any moment.

> Now unto him who is able to do immeasurably more than all we ask or imagine, according to his power that is at work within us, to him be glory in the church and in Christ Jesus throughout all generations, for ever and ever! Amen.
> —Ephesians 3:20–21

As you raise your level of expectancy, believe that you deserve God's best. You may have been waiting a while for your husband, depending on where you are in your journey toward marriage. Do not allow your desire to be married to cause you to settle for any relationship. Your heavenly Father wants the best for his children, and he knows exactly what you need. Trust God to write every aspect of your love story from beginning to end. You will discover that the husband he has for you exceeds your expectations and is better than you could ever make happen on your own.

Living your life day-to-day with expectancy allows you to believe in God's best, despite what is happening. Living your life day-to-day with expectancy provides space and opportunity for you to prepare to be the helpmate your husband will need. Living your life day-to-day with expectancy shifts your mindset and actions and positions you in closer proximity to God's promises.

Breakthrough

This is what the LORD says—he who made a way through the sea, a path through the mighty waters, who drew out the chariots and horses, the army and reinforcements together, and the lay there, never to rise again, extinguished, snuffed out like a wick: Forget the former things; do not dwell in the past. See, I am doing a new thing! Now it springs up; do you not perceive it? I am making a way in the wilderness and streams in the wasteland.
—Isaiah 43:16–19

In the final chapter of your love story, God will resolve the conflicts you encountered during your journey toward marriage. This resolve may not entail closure for every failed relationship that involves apologies from the men who hurt you along the way or their acknowledgment of the great woman you are. The conclusion of your love story will give you a much better gift, an understanding of why God made you wait, and how the experiences you endured were necessary to prepare you for the husband God had for you all along. This is the part of your love story that you have been praying for all this time. What was once a struggle will be effortless. Your breakthrough has finally arrived!

The reward you will receive for releasing control and trusting God to author every aspect of your love story from the development of characters to orchestrating the setting, plot, conflict, and theme is a beautiful resolution in which God will strategically place your husband in your life. When God believes you are ready to receive the husband he has for you, he will appear. It will not seem as though any time has been lost during the wait because your blessing will exceed your past disappointments. The level of favor you will receive from God will restore and increase your life far beyond what you have experienced.

We find this promise in Isaiah 61:7, and it states, "Instead of your shame you will receive a double portion, and instead of disgrace you will rejoice in your inheritance. And so you will inherit a double portion in your *land*, and everlasting joy will be yours." The man that God has for you will not be perfect, but he will be the perfect man for you. The man that God has for you will not complete you. The love of your heavenly Father has already made you complete. The man that God has for you will make you feel so special when he asks you the four-word question you have been waiting to hear, but what is more extraordinary is that your heavenly Father chose you first.

The tools provided in this book were shared to assist you with positioning yourself for a breakthrough during your journey toward marriage. Celebrate that you are an *overcomer*. In all your ways, acknowledge the *omnipotence* of God. Build relationships with *allies* who serve as a system of support. Allow your heavenly Father to control the *time* and shift the *seasons* in your life. Release control and *surrender* all to God. The *waiting* and *detours* will not be easy, but with God, you will find *contentment*, *purpose*, and *happiness*. Hold tightly to God's *promise*. Remain in *expectancy*, and your *breakthrough* is soon to come!

Part 4: Closing Activity

"Part 4" of this book highlights how God will resolve your love story with a positive outcome. Revisit the Launch Activity at the beginning of "Part 4," where you identified the primary character, setting, plot, conflict, and theme in your favorite love story (novel, movie, play, or musical). What was the resolution? How does the ending of your favorite love story connect to what you have discovered in Part 4 of this book?

Favorite Love Story Resolution	*Part 4 Connections*

EPILOGUE

I am an only child, but my extended family is quite large and tight-knit. Most of my family and friends are aware that I am not the greatest cook. My lack of cooking skills is not so much my ability as it is a reflection of my level of interest. Although I do not have a desire to cook, if I focused on improving my cooking skills, I believe I would be a much better cook.

A few of my first cousins and I created a Cookin' Cousins Competition, in which we each prepare a dish for the family to taste-test and select the best dish. The cousin who prepares the winning dish is crowned Chef Cuz until the next competition. I am sure you are thinking, *You have no business participating in this competition, and what does cooking have to do with this book?*

I participated in several Cookin' Cousins Competitions and never came close to winning. Actually, one of my dishes will forever be the center of many family jokes. On October 2, 2022, the battle was on again, and this time, each cousin had to prepare one ethnic cuisine and one dessert. Two dishes? You know, I was completely stressed! I decided to keep my dishes simple by preparing a slow cooker pesto chicken risotto and Oreo cookie balls. The competition was scheduled to start at 4:00 p.m.

- *The detour*—At 3:45 p.m., I tasted the risotto, and it did not seem like the recipe I used was coming together well. I was not sure if the rice had been over or undercooked. I was so confused and in need of help. Typically, I would ask my parents, but we had to prepare our dishes without assistance. I immediately prayed and asked God to lead and guide me. Although I was unsure, I made the decision to continue cooking the risotto and tried to remain calm.

- *The delay*—Several family members communicated that they were running late—four-fifteen, four-thirty, four-forty-five, five o'clock. Each time a family member's arrival was delayed provided more time for the risotto to cook. The longer it cooked, the better it tasted! The recipe indicated a certain amount of cooking time, but my slow cooker needed additional time for the rice to cook.

- *The deliverance*—I tasted the risotto right before the competition began, and it was finally ready! The flavors were well blended, and the rice was just right. Each of the ethnic cuisine dishes were served, and I could breathe a sigh of relief that the risotto was fully cooked. At the end of the competition, the judges announced the final scores for the ethnic cuisine and dessert categories. As I anxiously awaited the results, to my surprise, the slow cooker pesto chicken risotto received the second highest score! I could not believe it. The dish I thought would be an epic fail actually turned out to be delicious!

I shared this story because God's timing is perfect! I encountered a detour when preparing the risotto and was not sure what to do next. As you know, cooking is not my thing, so I could have given up. Instead, I prayed for God's direction. Although I was not confident in my decision to continue cooking the risotto, I trusted my heavenly Father to lead and guide me without worry or concern. When I let go of control, God allowed the delays to work in my favor. He not only provided more time for the risotto to cook but it came close to being the winning dish. In case you are wondering about the outcome of the dessert category, (drumroll please) my Oreo cookie balls were a big hit and for the first time I was crowned Chef Cuz!

The one thing I want you to take away from reading this book is to hold on to hope. Never give up on your desire to be married. You may have experienced heartbreak after heartbreak. Maybe it has been multiple years since you have been in a committed relationship. Men very seldom approach you when you are out. You could be older now and feel like too much time has passed. There are so many circumstances that can discourage you from believing that God has someone great in store for you. Please do not close the book on your love story. Keep turning the pages. Each chapter will get you closer to the husband God has for you.

FINAL: CLOSING ACTIVITY

Thank you for engaging in this book. I hope you discovered tools that will help you thrive in your singleness as you continue on your journey toward marriage. Thriving in my singleness is a daily focus, and I continue to remind myself of the tools and strategies included in this book. The final Closing Activity will require you to reflect on each of the four sections and create a plan to help you along your journey. Reflect on Parts 1–4, and identify areas you would like to *stop*, *start*, and *continue* doing.

START	
STOP	
CONTINUE	

MY MORNING PRAYER

Heavenly Father,

This is the day the Lord has made. We will rejoice and be glad in it.

I invite you into my life today to lead me,
guide me, and show me the way.

God, I don't know what to do, but my eyes are upon you.

Give me instructions, but do it your way. I believe
grace and mercy will follow me every day.

Today is the day for my situation to suddenly turn
around. In you, I will rest safe and sound.

Father, thank you for your divine favor and making
all things beautiful in my life. I know you are
preparing me to be a wonderful wife.

In Jesus's name I pray. Amen.

ACKNOWLEDGMENTS

I have to start by thanking my heavenly Father for giving me the courage and confidence to write this book. I was not sure if my ideas would be well received as an unmarried woman, but God equipped me with everything I needed to be able to share my message with other single women.

I am eternally grateful to my parents, Willie and Barbara Lawrence, who have been my rock, my foundation, and my support throughout my life. I would not be the woman I am today without you! I am blessed to have you as a beautiful example of a long-lasting marriage with fifty-six years, and counting. Thank you for showing me the reality of marriage is filled with ups and downs, but your commitment and love for one another withstands the test of time.

Finally, to all those who have been a part of my journey toward marriage, *thank you! Thank you! Thank you!* To my extended family (aunts, uncles, and cousins), your love and encouragement helped me come to terms with my singleness, more than you will ever know. A very special thanks to my circle of friends. Your deep discussions about relationships, inspirational text messages, comfort after a breakup, girl's night out events, and simply your listening ear have been the highlight of my journey. Thank you for being my *allies*!

ABOUT THE AUTHOR

Dr. Tawanda Lawrence is the senior director of teaching and learning at a school district located in a suburb west of Chicago, Illinois. Tawanda holds a doctorate degree in educational leadership from DePaul University, a master's degree in administration and supervision from Roosevelt University, and a bachelor's degree in music education from Eastern Illinois University.

Tawanda is passionate about sharing her message and experiences as a single Christian woman with other women who desire marriage. As a first-time author, Tawanda is looking forward to publishing more books and articles that inspire and encourage single women to release control to allow God, the supreme author, to write their love story.

Tawanda resides in Chicago, Illinois, where she is a longtime member of Fellowship Chicago Missionary Baptist Church and an active volunteer at the Greater Chicago Food Depository. She enjoys spending her free time with family and friends, traveling the world, attending concerts and sporting events, exploring diverse cuisine, and relaxing at the spa.